BOTTLE PAINTING GUIDE FOR BEGINNERS

Beginners guide on bottle painting, how to paint bottle and ideas for glass bottle decoration

Daniela Ambrose

Table of Contents

CHAPTER ONE

INTRODUCTION

A simple and enjoyable way to spice up the interior of your home is to paint on glass bottles. When you do it yourself, you can select a layout that is ideal for your theme and add a unique touch of personalization. The eco-friendly home design scene is all about acrylic simple bottle painting designs, which are frequently made from recycled glass from alcohol or milkshake bottles. They look lovely as gifts for loved ones as well as decorative accents for the home, such as flower vases or table centerpieces. Glass bottles and jars are incredibly useful items with a wide range of applications. Your home and kitchenware can be greatly enhanced and personalized by painting on glass. Additionally, many people are consciously choosing to use glass rather than plastic in order to follow sustainable paths. This book will teach you through painting glass bottles, preserving your painted glass bottles, and covering some other fantastic glass bottle decoration ideas.

STEPS FOR GLASS BOTTLE PAINTING PREPARATION

Your kitchen decor can be spiced up by painting glass bottles. Additionally, you can make bottle art to label food and preserves, hold a bouquet, and decorate your home with them. Before you begin learning how to paint on glass bottles, there are only a few preparations you must make. Start the process by choosing the glassware you want to paint based on the intended use of the finished item.

HOW TO CHOOSE AND PREPARE YOUR GLASSWARE

Most glass bottles and jars, like tomato sauce bottles or jam jars, can be recycled from old food products. We advise cleaning and reusing glass bottles that you already own, but you could also buy new glassware, such as Mason jars. Prior to beginning the painting process, it is crucial to thoroughly clean the bottles and remove any labels with hot, soapy water. For any sticky stains on the bottle, you can also use acetone or rubbing alcohol. Additionally, this will guarantee that the paint adheres to the glass and binds tightly.

Which type of paint is utilized for bottle art?

You can decorate glass bottles with a wide variety of paints. Which paint is used for bottle art, and which paint type is best? You could use spray paints, chalk paints, or acrylics. If you want to paint intricate designs on your glass bottle, acrylic enamel paint is advised. A premium acrylic finish with excellent coverage and quick drying properties is called acrylic enamel.

While it is still wet, it is simple to wipe clean. It is advised to use an acrylic pen or marker when painting text and fonts, especially if you lack much painting experience.

Organizing Your Workspace

When setting up your workspace for quick glass bottle painting, it's crucial to take this step. Because acrylic enamel paint can become quite overwhelming in small, enclosed spaces, make sure you are working in a well-ventilated area. Ensure that you cover your desktop with newspaper or plastic wrap as well.

Painting on glass surfaces and working on bottle art can be challenging at first. There is something incredibly wonderful about learning a new process and further honing your skill set, even if you end up making a bit of a mess and making a few mistakes along the way.

CHAPTER TWO

EQUIPMENT AND METHODS FOR SIMPLE GLASS PAINTING

Here is where you can begin experimenting with various supplies, equipment, and methods to produce a truly original glass bottle painting. Other mediums and embellishments that you could use include glitter, paper products, string, metallic paints, and just about anything else you can think of. Additionally, you can use a glue gun to make intriguing textures, or stencils to make intriguing outlines, layers, and repeat patterns. Another creative option is to paint the interior of your glass bottle by adding paint and swirling the container until the interior is completely covered.

STEP-BY-STEP GUIDE FOR PAINTING GLASS BOTTLES

You can learn how to paint glass bottles in this tutorial, along with the steps involved in getting ready to apply paint. You are encouraged to experiment and explore various techniques to bring your glass bottle decoration ideas to life even though these are only a few basic steps in the glass bottle painting process!

List of Equipment and Supplies

Before starting your acrylic bottle painting project, gather the following tools and materials once your workspace has been prepared and covered. For a bottle art painting, you don't necessarily need all of the supplies listed below, but you are encouraged to use what you have instead!

1. Glass jars or bottles

2. Warm water

Dishwashing soap, rubbing alcohol or acetone, paper towels or cotton balls, a pencil, thick paper (300 gsm), a craft knife, paintbrushes, a painting palette, an acrylic marker or pen, acrylic paints or acrylic enamel paint (wall paint), a spray sealant or varnish, stencils, a cutting board, and so on. The Krylon Workable Fixatif, which adds an additional seal layer to the paintwork for your bottle art painting, is the best, most reasonably priced sealant or varnish. Although fixatives offer a strong sealant layer, they do not guarantee that your paintwork will be protected from cracking or chipping. Preparing Your Glass Bottles It is always advised to clean and wipe down your glass materials whether you are using new or up cycled bottles. This will guarantee that the acrylic paint will adhere to the glass surface and translate well.

Step 1

Hot-water rinsing your glass bottles

Start off by giving your glass bottles a hot water rinse. Do your best to avoid getting the bottle's interior wet because doing so could affect how quickly it dries. To do this, submerge the bottle completely in a sink filled with hot water, being careful to keep the top of the bottleneck above the waterline.

Step 2

Dry Your Glass Bottles with a Cloth You can dry each bottle with a soft cloth to hasten the drying process. Before continuing with the next step, make sure your glass bottles are completely dry. You can move them to your workspace once they have dried.

Step 3

Use rubbing alcohol to clean and disinfect your glass bottles Use rubbing alcohol or acetone to clean and wipe down your glass bottles to make sure there are no traces of labels, dust, or sticky adhesive nail polish remove. Rubbing alcohol tends to spread quite well, so you will only need to use a tiny bit of it on the cotton balls or paper towels. Your glass bottles should be set aside to dry. This process ought to be quick.

USING TEXT AND FONTS TO WRITE ON GLASS

It is advised to loosen your hand by attempting to write and draw fonts and texts on a scrap of paper or extra glass bottles and jars before you start the process of glass painting on bottles. You might take advantage of this opportunity to look through your kitchen and label the items in your pantry. You will discover how to write clear text for quick glass bottle painting in the following few steps.

Step 1

Use an acrylic marker to check your handwriting in the

Test your handwriting to begin with on any open bottles or jars. Your best effort should be to loosely write the label in your preferred font style and capitalization in the center of the glass bottle while holding it with your non-writing hand. The best way to learn how to paint on glass bottles is to experiment and get used to working onto the glass surface.

Step 2

Complete Labeling Each Bottle with Labels

Write the required label for each jar as you go, working your way through them all. When drying the bottles, try to work methodically with plenty of space set aside. Set aside all of your bottles or jars to dry properly after labeling them all.

Step 3

Apply a Varnish, Fixative, or Spray to Seal the Labels

Use spray sealant, fixative, or varnish to coat and protect your writing so that your labels won't rub off easily. By adding an additional coat, this will prevent the text from smudging or fading. This does not imply that the paint is permanent, though. The glass bottles should not be washed or put in the dishwasher. Stenciling is a great technique to use if you are a beginner painter. Create Stencils and Patterns on Glass. You have two options for making stencils: either you draw them yourself or you buy pre-cut stencils online.

CHAPTER THREE
BASIC OUTLINE OF
STENCIL DESIGN

Step 1

By drawing the basic outline of your design with a pencil, you can prepare your stencil. It should just be a quick sketch of the picture you want to print and outline on the glass bottle. It is advised to use heavier, thicker paper so that it can be reused more than once and won't fall apart after a few uses.

Step 2

Start Using a Craft Knife to cut out the Stencil Design Using a craft knife that is razor-sharp and a cutting board, start pressing through the paper to cut out the stencil design. By adhering to the plan you've drawn in pencil, press and cut through your stencil. It might take some time to complete this step, so be patient and persistent in your efforts to create the desired result for your stencil design.

Step 3

Test Your Stencil First test your stencil on a scrap of paper by experimenting. Then, using a paintbrush and the color of your choice, go over the stencil with the brush until all of the spaces are filled with paint. To reveal the design's outline, carefully peel away the stencil, working from one side to the next.

Pick up a glass bottle and test your process once you are confident enough in your stenciling technique.

Step 4

Let Your Stencil Print Dry After you are satisfied with how your stencils look on the bottle or jar, set them aside to completely dry. If necessary, you can also add a layer of fixative. Acrylic Bottle Painting Now that you've experimented with a few different methods on glass, it's time to put your painting prowess to the test. With the intention of using the glass jar as a flower vase, the artist in this tutorial decided to paint a landscape scene on it. You are urged to use original artwork and show off your artistic flair by painting any scene or pattern you like.

Step 1

Put Down the First Coat of Paint

Mixing your acrylic paints is the first step. After that, pick up your glass bottle or jar and insert your writing-free hand inside. When applying wet paint, this will make it easier for you to handle the bottle. Apply your first coat of paint and go around the glass using a broad paintbrush or sponge. Make sure there is no paint on the bottle's base. Place the jar on the table with the bottom facing up and let it sit there for about 30 minutes to dry.

Step 2

Apply the Second Layer of Paint in

You can apply the second layer of paint after the first coat has dried and is no longer tacky. Put your hand that isn't used for writing inside the glass, and then start steadily painting the surface. If there are still streaks in some spots after the second coat has dried, go ahead and apply the third coat even though you shouldn't need more than two layers of acrylic. Next, paint the glass bottle's base and flip it over so the lid side is facing up to dry.

Step 3

Acrylic Bottle Painting is to Mix Your Paints. You can now begin blending your paints to create the color scheme you want. To create a striking glass painting on a bottle, it is advised to use a variety of colors and high contrast tones.

Step 4

Start Adding Additional Details to Your Glass Bottle Painting Begin by focusing on the side of your glass bottle or jar that is facing the front. Now start enhancing your painting with more details. You can paint the background layer first, and then any additional design elements, if desired. Before moving on to the next step, give the painted side time to dry completely.

Step 5

To flip the glass over and keep adding details. Turn the glass over and keep adding details to the side that is facing away from the viewer. Allow the glass bottle painting to completely dry after adding all the components you want to include in it.

Step 6

Apply a Few Layers of Fixative to Seal Your Glass Bottle Painting After your painting has dried, turn the jar while spraying steadily while holding your fixative spray a few inches away. To give your artwork the best protection possible, you are encouraged to apply two layers of sealant or fixative.

IDEAS FOR GLASS BOTTLE DECORATION

Glass painting can be used in a variety of ways on bottle surfaces. By adding embellishments like beads, string, glitter, buttons, paper cut-outs, fabrics, ribbons, and many other decorations, you can reuse glass and give it a special touch.

Gifts That Are Personalized

A bottle painting makes a wonderful gift for someone. You can choose a color scheme that you know the recipient will adore. A glass bottle painting makes a really wonderful gift because it takes time and thought to create something so unique and thoughtful. A painting created with acrylic bottles can serve as a focal point in your living room or kitchen. By painting the bottle in a variety of colors and adding fairy lights, you can recycle glass. This will change the bottle so that it can now serve as a reassuring light in a reading nook. labeling pantry items is as easy as using glass bottles.

Step 2

Finish applying labels to each bottle

As you work your way through all of the jars, write the necessary label for each one. Try to dry the bottles in a methodical manner with lots of space available. After labeling all of your bottles or jars, place them aside to completely dry.

Step 3

Seal the labels with a Varnish, Fixative, or Spray.

To coat and protect your writing so that your labels won't rub off easily, use a spray sealant, fixative, or varnish. A second coat will be added to stop the text from fading or smudging. However, this does not imply that the paint is irreversible.

You shouldn't wash or put the glass bottles in the dishwasher. When starting out as a painter, stenciling is a fantastic technique to use. Create patterns and stencils for glass. Stencils can be created in two ways: either by hand drawing them or purchasing pre-cut stencils online.

Step 1

Create a Basic Outline for Your Stencil Design

You can prepare your stencil by sketching the basic outline of your design with a pencil. The image you want to print and outline on the glass bottle should only be a quick sketch.

A heavier, thicker paper should be used so that it can be used more than once and won't disintegrate after a few uses.

Step 2

Begin Cutting Out the Stencil Design with a Craft Knife

Start cutting through the paper with a cutting board and a razor-sharp craft knife to remove the stencil design Press and cut through your stencil by following the layout you've penciled in. This step might take some time to finish, so be persistent and patient in your pursuit of the desired outcome for your stencil design. Test your stencil in Step 3 Start by experimenting with your stencil on a scrap of paper. After that, paint over the stencil with a paintbrush and your preferred color until all of the spaces are covered. Working from one side to the other, carefully peel away the stencil to reveal the design's outline. Once you are comfortable with your stenciling technique, take a glass bottle and test your procedure. Let your stencil print dry in step four. Set your stencils aside to completely dry after you are happy with how they appear on the bottle or jar. You can also include a layer of fixative if necessary. Bottle Painting in Acrylic Once you've tried out a few different techniques on glass, it's time to test your painting skills. The artist in this tutorial chose to paint a landscape scene on the glass jar with the idea of using it as a flower vase. We strongly advise you to use original art and display your artistic talent by painting any scene or design you like.

First, apply the first coat of paint.

The first step in using acrylic paints is mixing them. After that, pick up your glass container and put your hand that isn't writing inside. This will make it simpler for you to handle the bottle when applying wet paint. Using a large paintbrush or sponge, paint the glass all around in the first coat. Verify that the base of the bottle is unpainted. The jar should sit on the table with the bottom facing up for about 30 minutes to dry.

Step 2

Involves applying the second layer of paint

After the first layer of paint has dried and is no longer tacky, you can apply the second layer. Put your non-writing hand inside the glass and begin steadily painting the surface. Even though you shouldn't require more than two layers of acrylic, if there are still streaks in some areas after the second coat has dried, go ahead and apply the third coat. The glass bottle's base should then be painted before being turned over so the lid side is facing up to dry.

Step 3

In acrylic bottle painting is mixing the paints.

Now you can start blending your paints to get the desired color scheme. It is suggested to use a variety of colors and high contrast tones to produce a striking glass painting on a bottle.

Step 4

Start Adding More Details to Your Glass Bottle Painting in Start by concentrating on the glass bottle or jar's front-facing side. Start adding more details to your painting now. If desired, you can paint the background layer first, followed by any additional design components.

Give the painted side enough time to completely dry before moving on to the next step.

Step 5

Flip the glass over and keep adding details. Continue detailing the side that is facing away from the viewer by flipping the glass over. Add all the elements you want to the glass bottle painting and then wait until it is completely dry.

Step 6

Seal Your Glass Bottle Painting by Applying Several Layers of Fixative Holding your fixative spray a few inches away, turn the jar steadily while spraying after your painting has dried.

You are urged to use two layers of sealant or fixative to give your artwork the best protection possible.

Other Decoration Ideas for Glass Bottles

On bottle surfaces, glass painting can be applied in a variety of ways. You can reuse glass and give it a unique touch by adding embellishments like beads, string, glitter, buttons, paper cut-outs, fabrics, ribbons, and many other decorations.

Gifts with a Personal Touch

A bottle painting is an excellent present for someone. You can pick a color scheme you are confident the recipient will adore. Because it takes time and consideration to create something so special and thoughtful, glass bottle paintings make really wonderful gifts. Your living room or kitchen can feature a painting made from acrylic bottle fragments. You can recycle glass by painting the bottle a variety of colors and adding fairy lights. As a result, the bottle will change and become a comforting light for a reading nook.

THE END

Printed in Great Britain
by Amazon

24075645R00030